ISBN: 9798385893294

D1526582

Website: JadyAlvarez.com

Youtube Educational Videos: https://www.youtube.com/c/JadyAlvarez

Instagram: JadyAHomeschool

# Instructions

**Day 1** - Read the five sight words for the week and have the student repeat after you. After the student has practiced the words a few times, have the student complete the "Word Match" exercise.

**Day 2** - Have the student read the five sight words a few times without error in order and out of order. After the student has practiced the words a few times, have the student complete the "Find and Color" exercise.

**Day 3** - Have the student read the five sight words a few times without error in order and out of order. After the student has practiced the words a few times, have the student complete the "Trace and Write" exercise.

**Optional Activity** - Create flash cards using index cards to play bingo and other fun games. Use the cards to review current and previous words.

\* Remember to review the words by having the child read all of the words from the previous weeks from the Master List in the first page.

# Primer Master List

| Week 1 | Week 2 | Week 3 |
|--------|--------|--------|
| all | be | did |
| am | black | do |
| are | brown | eat |
| at | but | four |
| ate | came | get |

| Week 4 | Week 5 | Week 6 |
|--------|--------|--------|
| good | must | our |
| have | new | out |
| he | no | please |
| into | now | pretty |
| like | on | ran |

| Week 7 | Week 8 | Week 9 | Week 10 |
|--------|--------|--------|---------|
| ride | soon | too | what |
| saw | that | under | white |
| say | there | want | who |
| she | they | was | will |
| so | this | well | with |
| | | went | yes |

all

am

are

at

ate

# Word Match

| | |
|---|---|
| all | am |
| am | at |
| are | all |
| at | ate |
| ate | are |

# Find and Color

| all | am | are | at | ate |
|-----|-----|-----|-----|-----|
| blue | red | yellow | orange | green |

am

are

all

at

am

all

at

ate

ate

at

are

all

are

ate

am

# Trace and Write

all

am

are

at

ate

be

black

brown

but

came

# Word Match

be                    came

black                 brown

brown                 be

but                   black

came                  but

# Find and Color

| be | black | brown | but | came |
|----|-------|-------|-----|------|
| blue | red | yellow | orange | green |

brown

be

came

black

black

but

be

came

but

be

brown

black

but

came

brown

# Trace and Write

be

black

brown

but

came

did

do

eat

four

get

# Word Match

did                    eat

do                     do

eat                    did

four                   get

get                    four

# Find and Color

| did | do | eat | four | get |
|-----|-----|-------|--------|-------|
| blue | red | yellow | orange | green |

eat

get

did

do

four

do

did

get

four

eat

did

four

do

eat

get

# Trace and Write

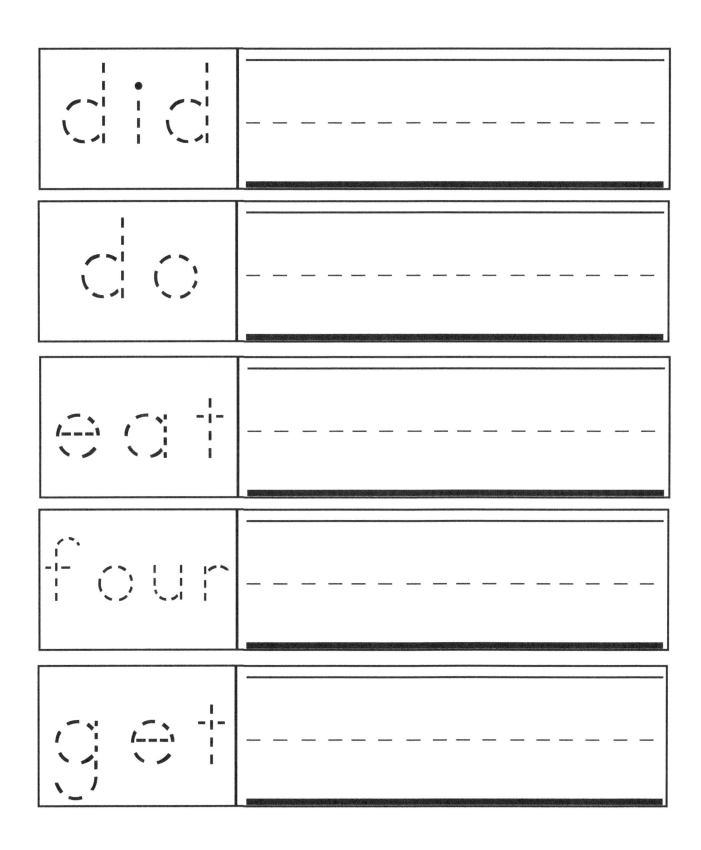

good

have

he

into

like

# Word Match

good                    have

have                    into

he                      like

into                    he

like                    good

# Find and Color

| good | have | he | into | like |
|------|------|-----|------|------|
| blue | red | yellow | orange | green |

into

good

like

have

he

he

good

into

like

have

he

good

into

have

like

# Trace and Write

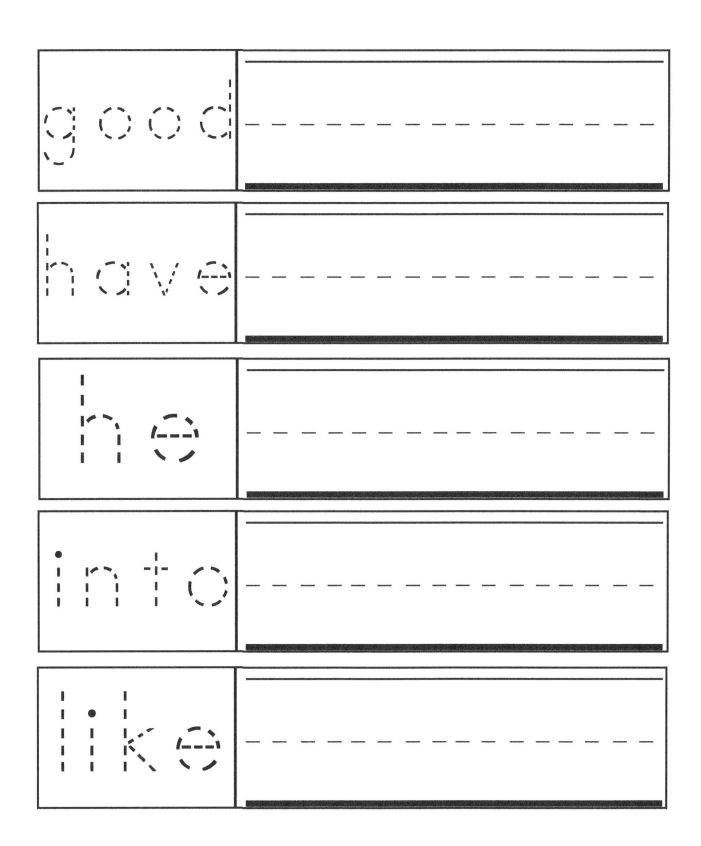

must

new

no

now

on

# Word Match

| | |
|---|---|
| must | now |
| new | no |
| no | must |
| now | on |
| on | new |

# Find and Color

| must | new | no | now | on |
|------|-----|-----|-----|-----|
| blue | red | yellow | orange | green |

must

new

now

on

new

no

no

must

now

on

must

no

new

on

now

# Trace and Write

must

new

no

now

on

our

out

please

pretty

ran

# Word Match

| | |
|---|---|
| our | ran |
| out | pretty |
| please | our |
| pretty | out |
| ran | please |

# Find and Color

| our | out | please | pretty | ran |
|-----|-----|--------|--------|-----|
| blue | red | yellow | orange | green |

ran

pretty

out

our

please

pretty

our

our

please

ran

out

please

out

pretty

ran

# Trace and Write

our

out

please

pretty

ran

ride

saw

say

she

so

# Word Match

| | |
|---|---|
| ride | say |
| saw | ride |
| say | she |
| she | saw |
| so | so |

# Find and Color

| ride | saw | say | she | so |
|------|-----|-----|-----|-----|
| blue | red | yellow | orange | green |

ride

say

so

so

saw

say

saw

she

she

ride

say

so

ride

she

saw

# Trace and Write

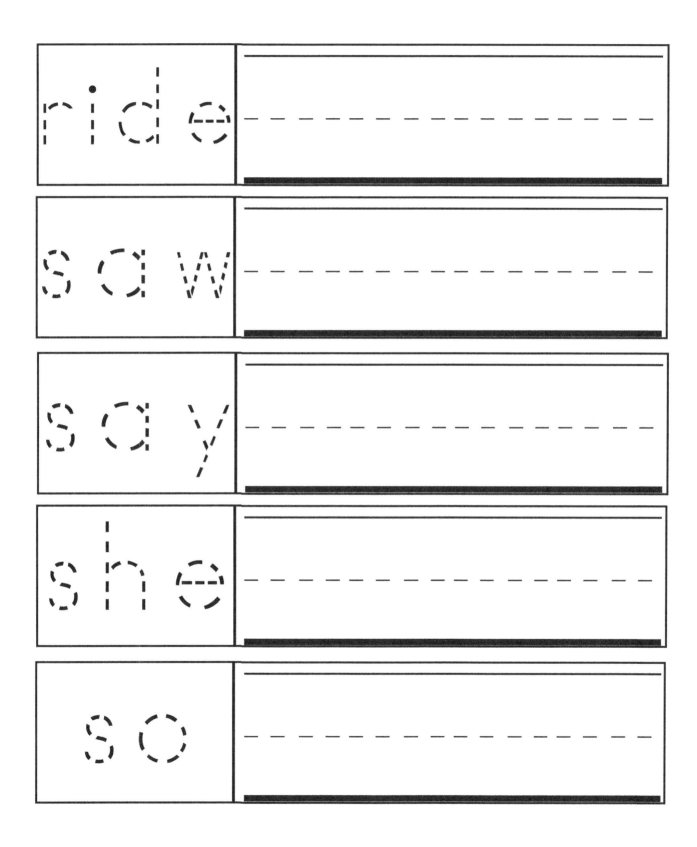

soon

that

there

they

this

# Word Match

| | |
|---|---|
| soon | this |
| that | they |
| there | that |
| they | soon |
| this | there |

# Find and Color

this    they

they    that    soon

there    soon

this    that    this

soon    they    there

there    that

# Trace and Write

soon

that

there

they

this

too

under

want

was

well

went

# Word Match

| | |
|---|---|
| too | want |
| under | too |
| want | well |
| was | under |
| well | went |
| went | was |

# Find and Color

| too | under | want | was | well | went |
|-----|-------|------|-----|------|------|
| blue | red | yellow | orange | green | purple |

too       want

well     went

well

want    under

under    went

went    too    was

was   want  well

too    was    under

# Trace and Write

too

under

want

was

well

went

what

white

who

will

with

yes

# Word Match

| | |
|---|---|
| what | who |
| white | what |
| who | with |
| will | white |
| with | yes |
| yes | will |

# Find and Color

| what | white | who | will | with | yes |
|------|-------|-----|------|------|-----|
| blue | red | yellow | orange | green | purple |

what        who

with        yes

with        who        white

white        what        yes

yes        who        will

will        will        with

what        white

# Trace and Write

what

white

who

will

with

yes

Made in the USA
Monee, IL
26 March 2023

30557650R00050